THE
BUSINESS PLAN
BLUEPRINT

MANAGEMENT · PLAN · TASKS · METHOD · TEAMWORK
COACHING $ · METHOD · VISION ?
ENTRAINEMENT · TRAINING · SOLUTIONS · IDEAS · STRATEGY

SHORTENING YOUR
BUSINESS' LEARNING CURVE

Terms and Conditions

LEGAL NOTICE

Table Of Contents

Foreword

A business plan is guidance, an important assistant for anyone who starts or runs a business. Business plans may consume some time to make them, but in the long term, you may save much time and cash flow. Get all the info you need here.

The Business Plan Blueprint

Shortening Your Business' Learning Curve

Chapter 1:

Business Plan Basics

Synopsis

You may need a business plan to apply for bank loans or getting investors for financial support. Here are some tips on writing a business plan:

The Basics

1. Create a vision. Before you get lost in details, start out with a vision or a mission statement. A mission statement should include values and a future view of your business.

2. Make an executive summary. Executive summary summarizes the whole business plan. Executive summary is necessary, as it is important to gain the interest of the viewers to continue looking at your whole business plan.

3. Include a description of your targeted market and services. This is essential to allow viewers to get a clear picture of what you are trying to sell or service. State it clearly in your business plan.

4. Include an analysis of the business environment and background. Do not expect viewers to understand what you are dealing with, even if your business is not a new idea. You may also review it anytime in the future for further adjustments.

5. Include a marketing and operation plan. Say it in the report how you will run your business. Include every details of it. Be clear and make sure your reports are easy to view.

6. Analyze your business competition. Find out all the detailed information you can get from direct or indirect competitors. Read about them from business magazines, newspapers, or get

resources from trading associations. Understanding competition is crucial to make a perfect business plan.

7. Finance planning. There is no business without involving finance. Be sure of your business financial status, and make clear reports about it. Justify your figures because a slight mistake may ruin your business plan, or your reputation in front of the viewers.

Chapter 2:

The Executive Summary

Synopsis

Executive summary is an introduction or an overview of a business plan. Executive summary gives the impression of the overall business plan. A business plan begins with the table of contents, followed by an executive summary. Even so, an executive summary should be the last paper you write as it summarizes the business plan according to the outline. These are some tips for executive summary writing:

Piece One

•   Remember that the executive summary is a summary. Try not to make it more than two pages. Make it about 2 - 4 sentences only for each business plan outline. Do not explain everything in detail because the executive summary is to draw viewer's attention to read more of the business plan.

•   Use proper and formal language. Do not be long-winded, but be strong and positive on your executive summary. Avoid using "uncertain" words. Instead of writing' our business may be successful in this area ', for instance, it would be better if it is ' Our business will be successful in this area'.

•   Include business name, location, selling products or services and plan purpose in the first part of the executive summary. The second part should include highlighted points of the business plan, or any important news that brings interest to the viewers, such as charts showing gross margin, expected sales and profits.

•   Be very sure of the purpose of the plan; if the business plan is for investors, do mention in the executive summary about the opportunities or benefits of investing in the business, investment amount required and what can the investors get from the business in return.

- Be in viewer's position to see if the executive summary is acceptable. Make sure it is smooth and fluent, and attracts attention. Find another person who knows nothing of the business plan to have a look at it and give comments. Add improvements before presenting it.

Chapter 3:

The Mission Statement

Synopsis

A mission statement is a statement of the business's purpose. Mission statements generally should be short and clear, thus easier for people associating with the business to keep that mission in mind and do what is best to achieve it. Mission statements should be updated over time to meet business' standard and needs.

What You Want To Achieve

Importance of a Mission Statement

• A mission could motivate people associating with the business to give better performance on progressing commitment. A mission statement will enhance their support, thus bringing greater positive outcomes for the business.

• Mission statements represent the business company or organization as a public image. Mission statements provide a set of progressive values, moral or ethics that incorporate with the business, thus it is a key influence for the business.

• People tend to stray away from their initial path of a business over time. Mission statements aid in setting goals to achieve and direct the business associates and partners to keep up with the initial business path.

• Writing a Mission Statement. Put the mission statement in a brief strong message, not exceeding one page. Some business plans would include a description of the targeted market, products and services standards in the mission statement. Mission statements usually also include expectations of profits and growth.

• Spend some time for the mission statement. It may be short, but it can mean a lot to the business company. Use some time to generate ideas on what to write, and what to include in the mission statement. Find out more on writing the best mission statement by reviewing mission statement examples by other business companies.

• Use creative words. Make it sound interesting with a smooth flow, to attract attention from the public or the viewers of the business plan; mission statements are meant to inspire action and create a dynamic image. Use colorful adjectives and verbs. You may consider adding in a glossary to describe terms used in the statement.

Chapter 4:

Exploring Financial Needs

Synopsis

Finance is important to set up a new business, or to upgrade business standards. One way to explore financial needs for business is through financial planning in a business plan. Financial planning helps managing expenses, controls spending and maximizes saving for an optimum budget in a business.

The Money

Financial plans come in three parts: income statement, cash flow projection, and balance sheet. Income statements are a statement of business profit or loss. Cash flow projection is a report describing cash flow in or out of the business. Balance sheet is a summary compiling the first two parts.

Tips on Writing a Financial Plan

• Be honest. Do not include reports with false statements. Do not try to impress viewers with overly expressive figures. An experienced business plan analyst can detect easily if there is any dishonesty in the plan. Justify your financial figures in exact or real situation. Say it as it is will bring more creditability to your business plan.

• Stay old-fashioned. Use standardized financial sheets, fonts. Stick with a black-and-white basic statement. Financial plans should be clear and easy to view. Adding too much spice, using shades or color fonts will do no good.

• Choose the appropriate accounting basis for your financial plan. There are two types: accrual basis or cash basis accounting. Accrual basis accounting records original transactions on a sale, not considering whether you received the cash. Cash basis accounting, on the other hand, records transactions on the day when receiving full payment by clients or customers.

- Be consistent. Use the same method for all accounts or financial reports. If not, it will confuse you and viewers of your business plan. Financial plans should be realistic, and contain factual information. Your financial planning will be accurate if you have done efficient research about it and present it appropriately on your financial plan.

Chapter 5:

Evaluating Competition

Synopsis

To start or run a business, one must identify competitors. Competitors may either ruin your business, or inspire your business to grow. In a business plan, one must include competition analysis, thus, understanding how well can your business grow in the market strategically.

Check it Out

Steps To Evaluate Competition:

1. Step 1- Find out about business competitors at a national level and your local area, especially within the business field you considered to enter. Information about them can be found also on websites, business magazines, trade associations, etc.

2. Step 2- Once you get to know about the competition; try to get more information about them, what they do, what they sell, and how they approach their targets. Read up about their business companies, associations, and more; if possible, read up about their annual reports- these are keys to their future plan. Understand their business backgrounds, products, targeting market, financial stabilities and support, and any other relevant news.

3. Step 3- Be conscious about indirect competitors of your business. Direct competitors are businesses similar to yours, but indirect competitors are businesses, in a way, in the same "field" as yours. You would like to run a pet shop. Direct competitors are other pet shops, while indirect competitors could animal clinics, animal hospitals or grooming services. In this case, the indirect competitors are pet services; they will not compete with you for business, however, with most of them around your business

location, you can be sure that pet care is in demand for that particular area.

4. Step 4- After evaluating competition and business competition; include this report in your business plan. This section of a business plan, competition analysis, can be offensive to other competing businesses but defensive for your own business. If the business plan is for investors, show in your competition analysis what you can offer or improve to benefit investors for investing in yours rather than in your competitors.

Chapter 6:
The Troubles You Can Run Into Without The Proper Business Plan

---

Synopsis

A business plan is important to keep you on track with your initial goals for business.

The Pitfalls

• You do not have a clear path. Without a proper business plan, you may run your business as it goes, soon you may find out you had run off track. You will forget your initial business goals and then do something new or have very different goals.

• You may miss an opportunity. Investors or banks for business financial support or loans mostly require a business plan. If you do not have a proper business plan, you will not gain the viewer's interest to invest or provide loans for your business.

• You may fail to prevent a failure. With less information, you may neglect a part of which contributes to great success of your business. When failure is approaching, reviewing an improper business plan will not help you to cope well with it, as you are not able to adjust the situation as soon as possible.

• You do not have an ability to foresee the future. Practically, business plans help you to start up a business with predicting the future and benefits your business may bring. If you do not have a proper business plan, you would probably not have a habit to think of the business in the long term rather than just seeing them in the short term.

• Your business will experience slow growth. People think having a business plan may restrict them from thinking out-of-the-box or having freedom to do as they like. However, without a business plan, how would you know your potential of bringing greater success to your business?

Wrapping Up

A business plan includes an executive summary, a mission statement, business description, environment analysis and background, financial plan, competition and market analysis, operation plan and any other attachments. Without a proper business plan you could get in trouble.

www.ingramcontent.com/pod-product-compliance
Lightning Source LLC
Chambersburg PA
CBHW041622180526
45159CB00002BC/982